# 40 DAYS
## TO A BETTER EMT MARRIAGE

## A FIRST RESPONDER DEVOTIONAL

# CHIEF SCOTT SILVERII, PHD

Copyright © 2019 Dr. Scott Silverii

All rights reserved. This book, or parts thereof, may not be reproduced in any form or by any means without written permission from the publisher, except brief passages for purposes of reviews. For information, address Blue Marriage™.

Dallas, Texas 75115

or visit our website at
www.bluemarriage.com

Five Stones Press

All Scripture quotations, unless otherwise indicated, are taken from the New American Standard Bible, ©1960, 1962, 1963, 1968, 1971, 1972, 1973, 1975, 1977, 1995 by

The Lockman Foundation. Used by permission. Other versions used are:

KJV—King James Version. Authorized King James Version.

NIV—Scripture taken from the Holy Bible, New International Version®. Copyright © 1973, 1978, 1984 by International Bible Society. Used by permission of Zondervan Publishing House. All rights reserved.

99 01 435769 987123 / 001 / 7643222

Printed in the United States of America

# DEDICATION

*Go Angels of Mercy*

*He who finds a wife finds what is good
and receives favor from the Lord.*
*~ Proverbs 18:22 (NIV)*

# TABLE OF CONTENTS

| | |
|---|---:|
| *Foreword* | xiii |
| *Introduction* | xvii |
| **Part 1 - Mission Briefing** | 1 |
| Day 1 - What is the 2:24 Unit? | 3 |
| Day 2 - Why Marriage? | 7 |
| Day 3 - Bulletproofing Versus Bulletproof | 11 |
| Day 4 - Leave and Cleave | 15 |
| Day 5 - Jealousy is Good | 19 |
| Day 6 - Sex in Marriage | 23 |
| **Part 2 - Preparing for Duty** | 27 |
| Day 7 - Am I Your Priority? | 29 |
| Day 8 - Budgets and Battles | 33 |
| Day 9 - Seeing Clearly | 37 |
| Day 10 - Spouse, Not Opponent | 41 |
| Day 11 - Have Sex | 45 |
| Day 12 - Got'cha! | 49 |
| Day 13 - Loose Lips | 53 |
| Day 14 - Safe Limits | 57 |
| Day 15 - What's Your Money Personality? | 61 |
| Day 16 - Blending an EMT Family | 65 |

# 40 days to a better EMT marriage

| | |
|---|---|
| **Part 3 - Danger Zone** | 69 |
| Day 17 - Choose Biblically | 71 |
| Day 18 - Secondary Trauma | 75 |
| Day 19 - Tickets to the Freak Show | 79 |
| Day 20 - Threesomes and Porn | 83 |
| Day 21 - What Does God Say About Sexual Sin? | 87 |
| Day 22 - Affairs and Temptation | 91 |
| Day 23 - EMT-on-EMT | 95 |
| Day 24 - Consequences | 99 |
| **Part 4 - Crisis Management** | 103 |
| Day 25 - The Game Changer | 105 |
| Day 26 - Power of Words | 109 |
| Day 27 - Forgiving EMTs | 113 |
| Day 28 - Fighting Fair | 117 |
| Day 29 - Friends Are Rare | 121 |
| Day 30 - Freedom and Forgiveness | 125 |
| Day 31 - Money Marriage | 129 |
| Day 32 - Boundaries for Family | 133 |
| Day 33 - Surviving Debt | 137 |
| Day 34 - I Forgive You | 141 |
| **Part 5 - Mission Accomplished** | 145 |
| Day 35 - Seeing is Achieving | 147 |
| Day 36 - Godly Loving | 152 |

| | |
|---|---|
| Day 37 - Active Listening | 159 |
| Day 38 - Leading Equally | 163 |
| Day 39 - Things Love Changes | 167 |
| Day 40 - Happily Married | 171 |
| *Afterword* | *175* |
| *Acknowledgments* | *177* |
| *About the Authors* | *179* |
| *Other Books by Scott and Leah* | *182* |

# FOREWORD

*He who finds a wife finds what is good and
receives favor from the Lord.
~ Proverbs 18:22 (NIV)*

I was first a medic in the military. It was what I'd wanted to be since high school. Naturally, I entered the world of EMTs as a civilian and was surprised to find that it was just as dangerous and personally devastating as my time overseas.

The difference was, I had married my high school sweetheart once I returned from active duty and the strain of the job was not only affecting me, but him too. Before I knew it, we were throwing the divorce word back and forth at each other until it no longer meant anything.

We both agreed to give it one last shot. We gave our lives and our marriage to Christ.

It was a mess honestly, and I never thought He could've done anything to clean it up. He did!

We're still married and going stronger than ever. It wasn't until we both stopped focusing on ourselves and started to focus on each other as our number one priority that our lives changed for the better.

It's tough out there, and I love you all for what you do, but you're no good to anyone else unless you're first good to you. Marriage is a great way to take care of you while caring for someone else.

God bless you and I pray your EMT marriage is amazing.

*Lacie Shaw-Perkins*
*Utah, USA*

scott silverii

# **INTRODUCTION**

Did you know that good marriages save more EMT's lives than a good IV drip?

It's true. The benefits of having a strong, healthy and happy marriage reduces the harmful effects EMTs face in terms of health, mortality and stress- related causes of death. Protected marriages also increase your overall happiness. A happy wife does make for a happy life. Guess what? Happy husbands also have better lives too.

Leah and I want to share 40 Days to a Better EMT Marriage. It worked for us, and we know it'll help grow your relationship into a rock solid marriage.

EMT Marriages Matter,
Chief Scott and Leah Silverii

# PART 1 - MISSION BRIEFING

# DAY 1
### The 2:24 Unit - What Is It?

*Therefore a man shall leave his father and mother
and be joined to his wife,
and they shall become one flesh.*
~ *Genesis 2:24 (NKJV)*

EMT Marriages are so important that God describes the very first marriage at the beginning of humankind. Genesis 2:24 describes the first and perfect bulletproof relationship between Adam and Eve. We call it the 2:24 Unit.

When you become one with your spouse, you place them and your marriage above everything else on earth. Yes, that means above the kids, the job, the friends and other family.

We can grow a strong relationship when we follow God's spiritual chain-of-command.

Honoring that heavenly hierarchy also means elevating your spouse so you both rise above anything that comes against you.

A 2:24 Unit provides marital strength and is the ultimate protection against addiction, affairs and all other threats against your relationship.

Your marriage will not survive in a house divided, but when the biblical model of a 2:24 Unit is honored, you're fighting back-to-back with your spouse and become tightly woven like Kevlar when shots are fired at either one of you.

The 2:24 Unit keeps life in perspective by balancing priorities. EMTs too often place the job above all else, but this isn't noble, nor is it the de- sign for marriage. When priority is placed on the marriage partnership, every other relationship becomes healthier.

Your happily ever after depends and begins with the 2:24 Unit.

EMT Marriages Matter

# CALL TO ACTION:

Describe your personal chain of command. The optimum structure would be God – then marriage – then kids – then family – then friends – then work, etc. But we realize that this is a goal and not the reality in every marriage.

Take the time to truly pray over what the chain of command in your life looks like. Once it's drawn out, pray over how that structure hinders or helps your marriage, and write out ways to realign priorities so that the reality matches your words.

# DAY 2
Why Marriage?

*The Lord God said, "It is not good for the man to be alone. I will make a helper suitable for him."*
*~ Genesis 2:18 (NIV)*

Marriage is an intentional arraignment created by God that allows us to enjoy relationship with each other. The relationship we share with our spouse is a direct reflection of the relationship God wants to enjoy with us. He adores us.

Believe it or not, we did not invent the institution of marriage. We may have messed it up a bit by leaving our vows on the church floor, but marriage remains sacred in God's eyes.

Marriage is a gift to, not a got too!

The connection between husband and wife was designed to sustain us throughout the days of our lives. God actually looked at Adam kicking it all alone and said that it wasn't good for him to be alone, so He created Eve, his wife (Genesis 2:18). Although there are tough times, the 2-as-1 marriage model creates an atmosphere where we've always got our best friend and eternal partner by our side and watching our back.

Marriage is also vital for your development in life. Alone, we turn inward and pursue selfish desires in an endless trial for self-satisfaction and fulfillment. It remains elusive.

Together, we learn to serve others above self. And, if children are included in the family mix, we really learn what it is to become a sacrificial servant. Investing in others makes us better in everything else we do.

God's gift of marriage is meant to be treasured and enjoyed.

EMT Marriages Matter

# CALL TO ACTION:

Make the time to talk about your lives as a married couple. Focus on the positives that you've each experienced since being married. Are there hard times? Sure, but now is the time to focus on the gift of marriage as God gave it to you. What do you love about being married?

# DAY 3

Bulletproofing Versus Bullet Proof

*Though one may be overpowered by another, two can withstand him. And a threefold cord is not quickly broken.*
*~ Ecclesiastes 4:12 (NKJV)*

Back in my rookie days I confused bulletproofing my first marriage with being bulletproof. Yeah, I was all into policing and about as deep blue as you could get. The job meant everything to me, and my marriage was primarily there to support me and get me back out on duty.

I'd come home, unload the junk from that shift on her, and then I'd head right back to work, the gym or to hang out with my brothers in blue. I had no clue she was suffering. She had no outlet for processing the drama bullets I'd just fired her way. I assumed if I was happy at work, she was happy in marriage. I was very wrong.

Protecting your marriage is a team effort. If one is hurting, you both are hurting. Unless you're both working similar jobs, there is an equity offset that usually manifests itself in the one-sided focus on healing. Both of you share the burden no matter what's going on.

Being in a 2-as-1 relationship means sharing the load no matter how heavy. You're both independently powerful, but together you are invincible to outside marital threats. Both of you must wear the Kevlar in this marriage, and that's built through focusing on each other's needs.

EMT Marriages Matter

## CALL TO ACTION:

The next time you bring work home and share it with your spouse, stop and ask them how they feel about what you just shared. Without giving them equal or greater time to talk about it, you are dumping the weight of your burdens on your spouse and then moving along without helping then to shoulder what it is that you created. Share – listen – respond – listen more – respond – listen even more – both are satisfied that all information was delivered clearly, understood accurately and processed fully.

# DAY 4

Leave & Cleave

*Therefore shall a man leave his father and his mother, and shall cleave unto his wife: and they shall be one flesh.*
*~ Genesis 2:24*

A solid EMT marriage is built upon the rock of an everlasting covenant. Covenants are not the same as a limited conditions contract. The example of this gift is shown to us through the very first marriage covenant between Adam and Eve. It's called the Leave and Cleave Clause.

Don't worry, leaving doesn't mean dropping your family or friends, and cleaving doesn't mean hanging on to each other's coat tails. It's a matter of relational priority setting.

Before I committed to making Leah my priority, I'd burned emotional energy on so many relationships that our own connection suffered. Eventually, all of those connections faded in and out, but my wife was left suffering in the wake of never knowing where I stood in our marriage.

God says nothing about friends, parents or in-laws as part of that meshing into one. Sometimes, parents have trouble letting go. That's why God said a man shall leave his mother and father…

That is an active term, not a lingering in between your spouse while clinging to mommy.

Your folks' job of raising you is over because that's a temporary assignment, but marriage was designed to last forever. Your parents have completed their mission of raising you once you become an adult.

It's time to leave mommy and cleave to your spouse. Your spouse must be the singularly most important person on this earth. Once I cleaved onto Leah, not only did it allow her to bask in the light of confidence in me, but also helped me balance the relationships with everyone else in my life.

EMT Marriages Matter

# CALL TO ACTION:

Discuss the realities of what leave and cleave look like in your marriage. Are you still living with one set of parents or family? Is it because of financial or housing reasons, or is it because of a lingering attachment or guilt of leaving? Identify attachments that cause stress, and discuss how to eliminate them so that your relationship can thrive.

# DAY 5

Jealousy is Good

*For the Lord your God
is a consuming fire, a jealous God.*
~ *Deuteronomy 4:24*

Are you willing to fight for your marriage? I mean really fight to win no matter what it takes to rescue it, maintain it or increase the level of intimacy to new heights. Being jealous of your 2:24 Unit is a good thing.

When the Bible talks about God being jealous, it's not what we associate with bad breakups. Righteous jealousy is protecting what's yours. And to be very clear, you each belong to the other, and deserve to be fought over; not fought against.

Once your marriage turns into a bulletproof 2:24 Unit, you do not belong to your friends, or squad, or that old flame back in high school. You are 2 people who choose to become 1 person.

We love this scripture (*Deuteronomy 4:24*) because it's an active, passionate consuming fire. Isn't that the way you both began the relationship? Nothing and no one stood in your way of getting to know each other. Fighting back-to-back against any foe. Focusing on your spouse ensures that the flames of marriage continue to burn.

But, righteous jealousy can easily turn ugly if secrets and suspicion are allowed into your marriage. Remaining close and transparent is the best way to avoid suspicions and grow as an invincible 2:24 Unit.

EMT Marriages Matter

# CALL TO ACTION:

Are there things, people, secreted confessions that cause unhealthy jealousy? It won't just go away. You both have to make an effort to share with each other what it is that causes disruption in your relationship.

Designate a time to talk about anything you feel that creates suspicion, jealousy or hurt. Agree beforehand that this is an information sharing and gathering time. No judgments, critical comments or conflict will occur. Just laying it out there for thought and consideration.

# DAY 6
Sex In Marriage

*Do not deprive one another, except perhaps by agreement for a limited time, that you may devote yourselves to prayer; but then come together again, so that Satan may not tempt you because of your lack of self-control.*
~ *1 Corinthians 7:5 (ESV)*

Are you having sex with your spouse? If you are, then amen. If you are not, then now's the perfect time to talk about it. Excluding medical conditions or unique situations, sex in marriage is vital to maintaining a great relationship. Isn't it funny that as hard as we try to get each other into bed before we're married, that sex is usually the first thing to go once we are married and say, "I do."

God's design for sex is a lifetime of pleasure and delight. Sex should be something we enjoy and look forward to in marriage. In a healthy relationship, there is effort and forethought given towards sex to make it amazing. However, satan's ultimate goal is that we will be ashamed of our sexuality so that we won't talk about sex with our spouse.

The good news is, you don't have to live a life full of frustration, shame and rejection. Through talking about important issues, we can overcome any obstacles preventing us from experiencing sex in marriage.

Sexual fulfillment works in the 2:24 Unit, but it doesn't come without active pursuit on the part of both of you. Sex and money are usually where we fail to communicate about issues. We'll talk the life out of something that happened on duty, but clam up in the bedroom.

Too often the simplest things erode into long-term issues and because sex is so vital to your relationship, it takes the brunt of the pressure. Never undervalue the importance of sex with each other. It's very, very important. Now, get out of here you crazy kids, and enjoy each other.

EMT Marriages Matter

# CALL TO ACTION:

How's the sex in your marriage? Are you still pursuing each other with the passion and vigor you once did? If not, then take this time to talk about it. Ask why or why not, and do not judge or accuse each other. Simply talk about the status of your marital sex.

# PART 2 - PREPARING FOR DUTY

# DAY 7

Am I Your Priority?

*The husband should fulfill his marital duty to his wife, and likewise the wife to her husband. The wife does not have authority over her own body but yields it to her husband. In the same way, the husband does not have authority over his own body but yields it to his wife. Do not deprive each other except perhaps by mutual consent and for a time, so that you may devote yourselves to prayer. Then come together again so that Satan will not tempt you because of your lack of self-control.*
~ *1 Corinthians 7:3-5*

It's not uncommon to naturally drift toward what interests us. Some lean toward career and achievement, while others focus on the home and family. There's nothing wrong with these pursuits unless they become your priority.

We've already talked about Genesis 2:24 where it says that the two shall become one. When you take someone as yourself, that's a clue that it's pretty important and deserves to be prioritized.

Priorities must be proven in real terms, not just words. One of our pet peeves is when someone says, "I love more than you could ever know." Why? Why can't you tell them, or better yet, why don't you show them?

During a rough patch in our marriage I was so focused on the goal of getting the job done. It was rare that Leah and I spent quality time together much less did anything special or out of our struggling routine. The more I misunderstood her sense of rejection as resentment, the more I pulled away because I though she didn't care about how hard my work was at that time.

The reality was, she didn't resent me, but she did suffer from being relegated to second to third place in my life. I wanted to put her on hold until I fixed the issues at work. But guess what? After that tough situation there was another tough situation, and so on and so on.

It wasn't until a confrontation caused me to stop putting her on ice while I rushed out to save the day, and returned to placing her first so we could resolve it together.

Our spouse is our priority in good times and bad. Even if it's your spouse that's causing the bad times, they must still be your priority. Here are some practical steps for ensuring that your spouse has no question beyond the shadow of a doubt that they are numero uno.

**Sacrifice** – "I will give this up for you."
**Time** – "I will spend quality time with you."
**Energy** – "I will meet your needs."
**Attitude** – "I want to be with you."

EMT Marriages Matter

## CALL TO ACTION:

Apply practical application to each of these ways of showing your spouse that they are the priority in your life. Write out ideas to put each of these four into action:

**Sacrifice – Time – Energy – Attitude**

# DAY 8

Budgets & Battles

*Jesus knew their thoughts and said to them: "Any kingdom divided against itself will be ruined, and a house divided against itself will fall.*
*~ Luke 11:17*

Budgets are not battle weapons we form for attacking our spouse. Setting budgets are mature conversations that reflect your values, goals, needs and dreams. Of course, conversations that never take place do nobody any good. Left in silent speculation, each spouse will come to question each other's intentions.

Money is one of the top three reason couples fight and divorce. It's usually during the divorce process that they finally begin to consider the role of money. That's because both are watching money march into their attorneys' pockets.

Let's not do that anymore. It would be such a wonderful accomplishment if we could put divorce attorneys out of business. Don't worry about them, they'll find another way to scrape by!

Setting a household budget is vital to the holistic health of your marriage. The stress caused by money is usually a result of failing to control your money. Trust us, if you do not control your cash, your cash will control you.

Also, most EMT couples who find themselves at odds over finances do not have a shortage of income. They have undisciplined spending habits. It took discipline to get through your training to save others. Now, use that discipline to protect your marriage and finances.

EMT Marriages Matter

# CALL TO ACTION:

Commit to sitting down with your spouse today and talking about setting a budget. You don't have to get into details at this point. Just start the conversation about setting a budget by explaining why it's necessary and how it will help strengthen your marriage.

# DAY 9
Seeing Clearly

*And though one can overpower him
who is alone, two can resist him.
A cord of three strands is not quickly broken.*
~ Ecclesiastes 4:12

Because you are an EMT Marriage, your time is already demanded by the agency, others on your shift or in your squad, the dispatcher, the community and everyone else who thinks that because of your oath they own a piece of you.

This should be enough reason to want to claim ownership of your relationship and create a meaningful vision statement to guide your relationship. This is similar to an operations plan.

Most of us get married and assume once the wedding bash ends, that's also the end of the process. The wedding was just the starter's pistol. You have a lifelong race to run with the best partner you'll ever have. But, to run that race with success you must lay out a path.

Too many couples bump into each other throughout the day and figure they'll work it out somehow. Meanwhile each are growing dissatisfied in their own lives and relationship. Why? Because no one has identified why it is that you are married and what it is that you both want the marriage to look like and accomplish.

The point is, without purposeful intentionality, you both are only existing as roommates. With God as the center of your relationship, you and your spouse create an unbeatable combination, or a cord of three strands.

You have the God-given authority to define who you want to be and what it is that you want to be. Want to be parents? Then write that into your vision statement. Want to travel the world? Then write that into your vision statement. Want to be a chief? Then write that into your vision statement. Want to remain married and never divorce? Definitely write that into your vision statement.

EMT Marriages Matter

# CALL TO ACTION:

Together, write out a vision statement for what it is that you both want the marriage to look like. Make sure that your personal goals are goals that you both agree on and that they are obtainable as a couple.

Do you want kids, college, promotion, early retirement? Write it all out as part of your marriage vision plan, and once you both have agreed in prayer, live it out.

# DAY 10

Spouse, Not Opponent

*A gentle answer turns away wrath,
but a harsh word stirs up anger.*
~ Proverbs 15:1

Growing a 2-as-1 marriage requires treating each other with respect and kindness even when you don't feel like it. We always hurt the ones we love is a cliché, but it is so because there's truth in it.

This doesn't make it right, but because we're close and connected, it's easiest to lash out without fearing greater consequences as might be found from a stranger.

Building a solid relationship where affirmation and uplifting are the core foundation takes effort. For most of us it doesn't come naturally, so learning to fight fair is a great place to start. Here are a few ways to make sure you don't turn your spouse into your opponent.

1. Start your sentences with "I" instead of "You" — "I feel frustrated when we're late" is easier to hear than "You always make us late."
2. Keep your fighting away from your kids — unless you model how to resolve it in front of them.
3. Stay clear of "character assassination" — don't assign negative labels to each other (e.g., "You're so lazy").
4. If you need a timeout, take it — but agree on when you'll come back.
5. Avoid expressing contempt by rolling your eyes or being sarcastic — it's toxic to your relationship.

EMT Marriages Matter

# CALL TO ACTION:

Many of us are used to taking statements or paying particular attention to what others say and how they say it. It's no different when we're married, except that we're the ones who usually fail to pay attention to our own words.

Try adding these 5 tips to your daily process, and open yourself up to the potential of improving your relationship by including positive words of affirmation. Even if you have to start by sending yourself a text each day to say, "Compliment him/her on their _____."

It'll launch a pattern of uplifting communication that helps you both become more willing to talk openly.

# DAY 11

Have Sex

*And God blessed them. And God said to them, "Be fruitful and multiply and fill the earth and subdue it, and have dominion over the fish of the sea and over the birds of the heavens and over every living thing that moves on the earth."*
*~ Genesis 1:28 (ESV)*

A happy spouse in the sheets makes a better EMT on the streets. The physical, physiological and psychological benefits of sexual intimacy in marriage not only keep you both connected, but adds marital protection to your 2:24 Unit.

Did you know?

**Less Stress** – married people have less dramatic responses to psychological stress. This becomes so important in combating the effects of PTSD.

**Richer** – married people experience per person net worth increases of 77% over single people. Married people also gained significantly more wealth than divorced people. Also, people who divorce in their 40's never recover from the financial loss.

**Safer** – married people take fewer risks; including substance abuse, and live happier, with better health benefits.

**Survive** – married people have better cancer survival rates than single or divorced.

**Live Longer** – marriage lowers the mortality rate for men by 80% and for women by 59%. Non-covenant living together actually reduces the lifespan.

There's no denying that a 2:24 Unit is better for both spouses' health, wealth and happiness. Don't deny one another the joy that God created for your pleasure.

BTW: despite popular belief, the Bible does not have a list of what Not To Do in your marriage bed. As long as it's mutual and pleasing to both of you, have at it!!

EMT Marriages Matter

## CALL TO ACTION:

Does sex take the shape of a weapon or reward in your marriage? It's time for both of you to have an honest conversation about the issues you may be having in your sexual relationship.

If adultery or porn addiction are present, stop pretending that it doesn't affect the connection. Talk about it to help the healing process. If need be, work with a Christian marriage counselor.

# DAY 12

Got'cha!!

*So then each of us will give
an account of himself to God.*
~ Romans 14:12

Part of strengthening your relationship involves adding layers of marital power through accountability. We know some people are resistant to this, but let's look at it through a hero lens for success in marriage.

Accountability is an honest reckoning of self-judgment. Your spouse should also be there to help monitor with an objective perspective, and gentle, encouraging words.

The negative connotation to accountability comes from associations to discipline. Back in grade school, on the job, civil and criminal codes, and in church, all we've ever known is the reactive nature of being held accountable.

No wonder no one wants to hold themselves accountable. When applied in a negative "gotcha," after the fact, it loses its appeal and application for the sake of what good we're working to accomplish.

What if we instead looked at accountability in a positive light? If instead of it being a tool to retro-discover failures, we front-load success by clearly identifying the expectations ahead of time, and then apply accountability measures as a means to progressively monitor and guide the entirety of the marriage journey.

EMT Marriages Matter

## CALL TO ACTION:

Create a list of proactive accountability measures and attach incentives with them. If accountability is required because one or both have fallen to sexual temptation, then make sharing all social media account passwords a measure to ensure ahead of time that you will not be tempted to send or accept potentially destructive messages.

# DAY 13

Loose Lips

*However, let each one of you love his wife as
himself, and let the wife see
that she respects her husband.*
~ Ephesians 5:33

EMTs use the excuse, "They just don't understand what I go through." Ever used that one? I've never been to the moon, but it doesn't mean I wouldn't love to listen to an astronaut talk about space exploration. It's the same thing with EMT couples.

There's no reason to withhold from each other. This doesn't mean a massive data dump when you walk through the door after duty, but it also doesn't mean you should prevent them from the opportunity to share the events (good and bad) in your life.

I can guarantee you're telling somebody about what happened on duty. It might not be your spouse, but you are talking to a civilian. It's naturally how we process. The reality is, whoever that person is, even if it's your high school bud or your parents, they are not your spouse.

Committing to grow a rock solid 2:24 Unit means placing your spouse as your priority. They will be there long after your partner transfers or that civilian confidant no longer needs you for favors.

If you complain that your loved one doesn't understand what you're going through, it's only because you've chosen to stop them from doing so. Fill them in on the good and the bad, and then work together to process it as a 2-as-1 marriage.

EMT Marriages Matter

# **CALL TO ACTION:**

Talk with your spouse about what levels of sharing each feel comfortable with as it relates to your careers. Some people want to hear the details, while others would prefer to only know you are okay.

There's a difference between rehashing and processing. Set boundaries to ensure that the lines of communications remain open without cluttering them with locker room gossip that only continues the drama of the moment without providing for a productive result.

# DAY 14
Safe Limits

*It teaches us to say "No" to ungodliness and worldly passions, and to live self-controlled, upright and godly lives in this present age,*
~ *Titus 2:12*

The protective limits you both need to set to secure your 2-as-1 marriage will be particular to your own situation. But those protections must be discussed and very clearly identified. They are dividing lines that mark areas of access, protection and risk. There can be no security in misunderstood limits.

For example, if there has been a history or potential for infidelity, then those limits might include restricting/blocking access to the third party through social media, work place, etc.

An issue such as overspending and breaking the family bank might include guidelines such as budgeting, and both spouses approving expenditures over a certain dollar amount.

The protections you establish to guard your 2:24 Unit will be as varied as your personalities, so take time to explore and set meaningful boundaries not to punish, but to protect.

Will it be a piece of cake knowing there are limits to selfish desires? No, because satan wants you to cross that forbidden line. He can't shove you across it, but he will try to get inside your head to consume your thoughts with nothing else but what's been set outside your safety zones. Don't buy into it, he's the father of lies.

This is why we want you to understand there is security and joy within your own established guidelines. We set safety distances between ourselves and the public for our protection, why not give our marriages the same security?

EMT Marriages Matter

# CALL TO ACTION:

In writing, list protective limits for each of you. They will vary depending on your circumstances. If it's overspending, maybe the boundary is no purchases unless both agree up to a certain dollar amount. If it's being gone from home to hang out with your partners, then designate those times or ensure they include your spouse. Don't leave anything out because you're afraid of missing out on something beyond the protective limits of your marriage.

# DAY 15

What's Your Money Personality?

*For which of you, desiring to build a tower, does not first sit down and count the cost, whether he has enough to complete it?*
~ Luke 14:28

**K**ids, cash and sex are the top three stressors in marriage. Yes, they can cause your marital strength to fray faster than a medi-pouch inside your ambulance on a hot summer day. Understanding spending motives adds protection to your 2:24 Unit's relationship.

There are generally four types of languages spoken by our respective money personalities according to Pastor Jimmy Evans;

1. **Driver** – Money means success, self-esteem and security.

2. **Amiable** – Money means love by buying and sharing to show affection.
3. **Analytic** – Money means strength, and keeps away chaos.
4. **Expressive** – Money means acceptance and respect as basis for relationships.

Looking at these types of money languages, you can see how vital each one is for understanding the way we not only think of money, but how it plays an important role in our lives.

Leah and I both grew up poor, and as a result of our respective experiences, we approach money very differently. I save money because it meant security. Leah spends it to show others love. Either extreme was not good, so we learned to balance out our strengths.

It's okay if you both practice a unique money language, because the variance helps balance the budget. Where the differences are agreed upon is within the context of a written budget.

Avoid the debt, and the fighting by being pro-active in discussing money management through a monthly budget. You might even find you have the extra cash to go do something fantastic for each other.

EMT Marriages Matter

# CALL TO ACTION:

You and your spouse are going to gain financial freedom by taking control of your money. Before you move into the season of budgets and new confidence over finances, have a conversation about your money personality.

Talk about what it is, how it began and what it means to you. Also, discuss ways to blend the differences in your two personalities so that the marriage eliminates one of the big three hot buttons between couples – Money!

# DAY 16

Blending an EMT Family

*We do not dare to classify or compare ourselves with some who commend themselves. When they measure themselves by themselves and compare themselves with themselves, they are not wise.*
~ *2 Corinthians 10:12*

Don't compare your new marriage, family, life etc. to the one you had before. It's new territory. It's not a first marriage/first family situation. Don't treat it like one. And don't let your extended family do it.

How many times in your marriage have you heard a family member or friend say, "Well, when he/she was married to (fill in the blank)…"

Comparison is the thief of joy. Unfortunately, we do it more than anyone else we know. Sometimes, we don't give second chances at love the respect they deserve or look at a new marriage as a consolation prize because it was born out of failure from the first. You have a choice in deciding to prioritize your marriage instead of comparing it. Choose wisely.

You've both got a past and it's important to be honest and upfront about it. You both must be receptive in talking about it whenever triggers or issues come up. This goes whether you're a widow/widower or have been divorced.

Issues are going to come up. Ignoring them only prolongs the agony. Talking about it begins the healing process. Growing a 2-as-1 marriage requires a commitment and communication—not comparison.

EMT Marriages Matter

## CALL TO ACTION:

If your marriage is a blended family, have you both talked about exactly what that involves? Are there ties to a first marriage through feelings (positive or negative), property, financial obligations or time? Every strand that tethers either of you back to the past is a potential harm to the current and future. Identify the risks and minimize where you can.

# PART 3 - DANGER ZONE

# DAY 17

Choose Biblically

*Husbands, love your wives, as Christ loved the church and gave himself up for her.*
*~ Ephesians 5:25*

Growing a powerful 2-as-1 marriage is a choice. What God created to last forever is not dependent on your mood from one day to the next. There is a choice to love or not to love because believe it or not, love is not an emotion. It's a decision.

People may claim to "fall out" of love, but that's a cop-out. You choose to no longer love your spouse, or you can also choose to always love them.

With the reality of choice, divorce should not be an option. Actually divorcing because you claim to have fallen out of love is like selling your gun because you ran out of ammo!! Instead, reload and decide to focus your love where it belongs - on your spouse.

Yep, reload your love through attention paid to your spouse. Not the job, the next promotion or the new assigned cruiser—your beloved spouse deserves your focused attention.

It's a choice you get to make, so make the right one. A 2:24 Unit is also a choice to place each other above everything and everyone else. Together, your marriage will become protected, but you must choose wisely.

EMT Marriages Matter

## CALL TO ACTION:

This is a simple act, but possibly the most important choice you'll both make. Tell each other that you will not divorce and mean it.

# DAY 18

Secondary Trauma

*Fear not, for I am with you; be not dismayed,
for I am your God; I will strengthen you,
I will help you, I will uphold you with my
righteous right hand.*
~ Isaiah 41:10 (ESC)

Placing ourselves on society's frontline means we become trauma sponges. We run toward danger without an expectation of thanks, but we never expected the toll it would take on our lives.

To remain on the job, we learn to process, cope or suppress the trauma. Being an active participant in resolving the traumatic scenario is helpful to a degree for the hero. Our spouses don't have that same opportunity.

It's easy for them to take on secondary trauma. I used to tell Leah details of everything from murders to adversarial city council meetings. I didn't realize the damage it was causing her. I was actively engaged in the conflict, so at the very least, I was able to process the threats through action.

Leah was trapped with only the information I shared and no way to process it. You may have found yourself in that same situation of your venting causing your spouse harm long after you've hopped to the next radio call for service.

It's important that when we open up to our spouse, we also allow them the time to process it and then discuss it or ask questions to gain a better understanding of what it was that you experienced, and how it was resolved.

## CALL TO ACTION:

Before sharing or venting about what happened on duty, promise your spouse that after you say whatever's on your heart, you will wait and hear what's on theirs. And, while your spouse is responding to your emotional unload, promise not to interfere, correct or criticize them.

# DAY 19

Tickets to the Freak Show

*Besides, they get into the habit of being idle and going about from house to house. And not only do they become idlers, but also busybodies who talk nonsense, saying things they ought not to.*
~ 1 Timothy 5:13

Growing a solid 2-as-1 marriage means you and your spouse focus on each other even when times are tough. Going outside of that very small circle only invites trouble into your lives. Your family, in- laws and friends may love you, but they will never, ever care about your marriage like you do (or you should).

You and spouse are most often the ticket that in-laws need to attend the freak show. Phone calls to family criticizing the spouse empowers them to butt in. And by getting involved, that also includes taking sides and even suggesting divorce. If you want family out of your business, be careful how often you invite them into it.

If your in-laws know as much about your relationship as you do, then there's a problem between you and your spouse. They shouldn't know each argument, major purchase, child issues, etc.

Forgiveness between a husband and wife should be a continuing process. But parents, families and friends tend to hold grudges against anyone who offends their loved one. We've seen parents bring up food tabs from the wedding reception over 20 years prior. Keep your partner's back by not talking behind it.

EMT Marriages Matter

## CALL TO ACTION:

Discuss the importance of keeping your business, your business with each other. When a man feels his words are betrayed, he will rarely share again. When a woman feels insecure about sharing her heart, she'll begin to distance herself. It's vital that you both have a trusted space to share anything without family or friends being told or asking for advice. If telling others is an issue or one feels it's a necessity, then discuss why they feel the need to spread the word and work to resolve the leak.

# DAY 20

Threesomes & Porn

*But since sexual immorality is occurring, each man should have sexual relations with his own wife, and each woman with her own husband.*
~ *1 Corinthians 7:2*

Connected and committed is the way God intended you to share your life, and also your marriage bed. It's so important to understand that Genesis 2:24 is the foundational rock upon which marriage is based.

The model of 2 becoming 1 is not just a spiritual reference, but is a physical requirement as well. There is no justification for including anyone else in the process of the two of you coming together sexually.

The process of building your marriage into a bulletproof team does not allow for including others in your married sex life. Whether it's another person or pornography, it violates the core of God's Word in Genesis.

Mental and emotional adultery is just as destructive as the flesh. When you go outside of the attraction your spouse brings, it's an offense to the gift that God created just for you.

When you break the rule, then you separate yourself from grace and begin to operate on your own. Yes, even operate apart from your spouse. While you might think they don't even know about your violations, trust us, when you peel tape from paper it's impossible to function independently and without harm to each side.

Once you come together as husband and wife, there is no going back to operating independently without consequences.

EMT Marriages Matter

# CALL TO ACTION:

Pornography is so pervasive in our culture that it's hard to imagine a married couple that hasn't had to deal with some aspect of it. Porn isn't harmless or healthy for your sex life. If one or both of you are having an issue with pornography, have an honest conversation about why it's needed or desired. Talk about the negative ways it affects one or both of you and make a commitment to keep the marriage bed safe from outside forces.

# DAY 21

What Does God Say About Sexual Sin?

*Marriage is to be honored by all,
and husbands and wives must be faithful to each
other. God will judge those who are immoral
and those who commit adultery.*
~ Hebrews 13:4

Let's look at the key scripture, and you tell us what you think God is trying to say. The sanctity of marriage is affirmed in Hebrews with a very straight forward and powerful word about sex and sin.

I'm not sure about you, but as far as marital sex advice goes, it doesn't get much better or simpler than that. Keywords from this verse that jump out at me are; *honor – faithful – judge*.

In the hero life, these words are key descriptors of what we do, and how we feel about doing the job. If we're willing to lay our life down for strangers based on these key terms, then why can't we lay down our temptations for sexual sin?

God's not boring or dull or only found on the dusty pages of a book in the drawer. He is alive and active in our lives to the extent that we allow Him to be. Sex was created to be enjoyed and the special connection that pulls a husband and wife together. Any other way, and we're just wrong.

EMT Marriages Matter

# CALL TO ACTION:

We want you to know that even if sexual sin has caused damage in your marriage that God loves you both and wants you to be restored. Marriages can survive and thrive after an affair or other sin offenses.

Forgiveness, repentant hearts and a willingness to remain together and repair, rebuild and restore your relationship is possible. But, it begins with confession and forgiveness. Pray about sexual sin and ask God to give you the words to confess to your spouse. It's tough but this is the only way to know the peace of forgiveness.

# DAY 22

Affairs & Temptation

*Flee from sexual immorality. All other sins a person commits are outside the body, but whoever sins sexually, sins against their own body.*
~ 1 Corinthians 6:18

Affairs don't start in the bedroom. They start with a glance, and a returned look. A longing stare at their body and an acknowledgement that it's pleasing to see, and a stimulation to the fantasy of thought.

Affairs come to fruition because the married offender is conceited with a prideful spirit into thinking it's okay this one time, their spouse will never find out, or God will forgive them.

Is living the shady life that important for filling a void in your spirit? If so, there's much more going down than an overactive sex drive. There is no peace in darkness, but there is pleasure in the light of purity and a vibrant, healthy sex life with your spouse.

We love the old saying, "If the grass is greener on the other side, then it's time to water your own lawn." It takes discipline, sacrifice and self-control to live and strive in the EMT life.

These are the same personal qualities to remain committed to your spouse. If we're going to be heroes, then that goes without stopping. It's not a hat we can take off or put on to fit the situation. It's part of who we are.

"Yeah, but it's hard with all that temptation." You might say. It's only hard if you allow the circumstances that create temptation. The best way to handle it is found where else? God's word.

EMT Marriages Matter

# CALL TO ACTION:

Accept that temptation is a part of life. It happened in the most perfect setting in all of human history (Garden of Eden), and it will happen with all of you. Temptation takes on many forms, but sexual sin is one of the most destructive to marriages.

Take a personal, emotional and spiritual assessment to determine if you have or might encounter relationships that are leading to an affair, or cloud your thoughts with temptation. Pray God takes the desire out of your heart for that other person, while renewing the passion for your spouse.

# DAY 23
EMT-On-EMT

*Brothers will turn against their own brothers and hand them over to be killed. Fathers will hand over their own children to be killed. Children will fight against their own parents and will have them killed. Everyone will hate you because you follow me. But the one who remains faithful to the end will be saved.*
~ *Matthew 10:21-22 (ERV)*

The depth of hurt within the medical fraternity astounds me. Hurt people, hurt people. Pain and unforgiveness travel across multilane expressways within the ranks. Unfortunately, there are no caution signs or stop lights as we hate and hurt out of control until we crash.

It's an alpha-environment, where the wolves devour sheep even if they wear the same uniform. The uniqueness of EMT culture is that we bond together to fight the external enemy, but when none exist, we cannibalize each other.

It's constant drama in the briefing room. Whether it's about preferential assignments, who got the primo bus, grant OT or whose sleeping with who, it gets messy. Guess what? We bring it home to our spouse, and usually project what we've endured onto them.

This is where the jabs go just below skin deep, so anger and resentment build up, but not bubble over. Instinctively we suck it up without confronting each other because we're heroes, and that's what we're supposed to do, right? All that does is create a wounded spirit. We then become what? Hurt people.

EMT Marriages Matter

## **CALL TO ACTION:**

Talk to your spouse about any situation with a co-worker that is causing you anger or stress. Drop the facade of being iron-skinned. Allow yourself to be vulnerable with your beloved. They know you and love you more than anyone on your job. Talking about strained relationships helps you process the hard feelings you may have against co-workers and thus help you be not so affected when they try to pounce.

# DAY 24

Consequences

*For the wages of sin is death, but the free gift of God is eternal life in Christ Jesus our Lord.*
~ Romans 6:23

On the most basic level of life there are decisions and consequences. If we eat ice cream, we get fat. If we are attentive to our spouse, we get intimacy. See how that works?

If your relationship has reached the low point where consequences for your destructive actions no longer matter, it's time for intensive focus because you're dealing with issues that began much earlier than your marriage.

Consequences have no influence when past personal pain is so intense, and the need to numb it is so strong that you almost find yourself wanting to get busted in hopes it goes away.

We get to a level where we've been hurting for so long that no consequence short of death could make us feel any worse about ourselves. That's a very dangerous place to be. It's also where addictions and abuse are waiting.

How do we know there are such serious past pain issues that may be manifesting themselves into problems that are only now hurting your marriage? It's usually when accountability and boundaries are established that these darker issues come into the light.

Please take this as a positive encouragement for setting boundaries and placing accountability systems in place. Otherwise, it would be like avoiding the doctor because your arm got chopped off. Avoiding is not healing.

While you may be immune to the harsh effects of negative consequences of your behavior, your spouse, family and loved ones are not. They suffer like you do, except they feel the pain.

Heal and know peace!

EMT Marriages Matter

# CALL TO ACTION:

Write out a list of three negative events in life that were a result of your bad decisions. This isn't to cast shame, but to illustrate the reality of how directly linked your choices are to consequences. Now think through or discuss how different each of the three scenarios would have been as they affected your life.

# PART 4 - CRISIS MANAGEMENT

# DAY 25

The Game Changer

*Be kind to one another, tenderhearted, forgiving one another, as God in Christ forgave you.*
~ *Ephesians 4:32*

If there was only one thing you both had to change to help develop a 2:24 Unit, it would be to start praying together. Not praying just before meals or at a holiday gathering, but going before God in prayer daily.

When times get tough, we usually go ghost or force our way into the situation without fully understanding the underlying circumstances. Either way, the over or under response usually ramps up the initial issue.

Moving into active and expectant prayer will do more for your 2:24 Unit than buying roses and rings. Failing to pray together is an unproductive response to an ongoing situation. This isn't a case of letting sleeping dogs lie. Get in the fight.

Armor up with the word of God and allow Him to defeat all of your enemies who stand against your EMT marriage. God will bless your marriage for your faithfulness to prayer.

In order to build a truly 2-as-1 marriage, you must pray together. It changes everything from the way you speak to each other to the way you treat each other. I'll share that I have a "take charge" tendency that doesn't always come across as kind. Once Leah and I began praying together, I understood the power of loving speech.

Men as the God ordained head of the home should take the point on this assignment. Yet, seldom do men feel comfortable starting the practice of prayer.

## Here's How to Start Praying Together:

- Keep your prayers casual
- Schedule a set time each day
- Keep your prayers short but to the point
- Don't worry about memorizing Scripture
- Open your mouth and your heart will follow
- Ask your wife if there are prayer requests
- Be sensitive to the Holy Spirit's presence

EMT Marriages Matter

# CALL TO ACTION:

If you are not praying together, then start doing that. If you are praying together, press deeper into prayer and begin writing out a prayer request list.

# **DAY 26**

Power of Words

*But I tell you that everyone will have to give
account on the Day of Judgment
for every empty word they have spoken.
For by your words you will be acquitted,
and by your words you will be condemned.
~ Matthew 12:36-37*

We may not realize the power of each spoken word, but our spouse does. It either uplifts or cuts them clean to the core.

First responders encounter people who by the very nature of what they say may be understood as a threat against our wellbeing. They can be charged with a criminal offense, yet, when we use the very same context toward our spouse, we don't consider the severity of what was said against them.

Your spouse is not the enemy or some street-level encounter. Married couples should not measure individual successes by arguments won and lost. Both lose when confrontation becomes the standard.

Wasted words also have eternal consequences. If couples could witness this holy judgment like they watch episodes of #LivePD, there would be less negative, hurtful words spoken to each other.

And, while we're thinking through the verse above, please review everything you've said to your spouse in the last 24 hours. How about the last 12 hours, or more realistically, the last few hours? How would you be judged — condemned or acquitted?

Just as we learn the laws as to not break them, we too can learn or relearn to speak positive, affirming words to our spouse. When we truly see our spouse in the context of God's gift to us, there's no desire to demean or harm that gift through negative communications.

Forgiveness, affirmation and understanding will help you avoid the marital autopsy. Learning to say, "I'm sorry," also defuses lots of hot situations.

EMT Marriages Matter

# CALL TO ACTION:

Commit to focusing on what you say to your spouse. Set the timer on your phone for one hour, with the reminder to record your words. Only your words, not theirs.

After the timer goes off, start writing out strong, aggressive and hurtful words you used while talking to your spouse. Then decode the pattern of your speech as to whether it's similar to street and locker room talk or positive speak that uplifts your spouse.

# **DAY 27**

Forgiving EMTs

*For if you forgive other people when they sin against you, your heavenly Father will also forgive you. But if you do not forgive others their sins, your Father will not forgive your sins.*
~ *Matthew 6:14-15*

Let's talk some more about forgiving and how it relates to EMTs. Well, in this case, forgiving applies to us just the same as it applies to everyone else. It's non-negotiable, and we can't outwork it or fix it. We can't stress how important the active process of forgiving is.

This is a gift from God, and we'll not, and I repeat, we will not ever know freedom until we forgive those who have hurt us. Forgiving is about freedom. Your freedom; not the offender's freedom.

Forgiveness gives you the power to break the chains that bound you into torment, anger, hatred, or the hell of victimization. God gives you the ability to regain power through surrendering to His command of forgiving.

Some see it as weakness, and that's an unfortunate mistake. Forgiving is about having the authority to exercise control over your life. Part of that control is that once you have truly freed yourself from the hurt caused by someone, you now have the authority to determine the degree of relationship you'll have with that person. Forgiveness does not even mean reconciliation unless you want it. But, unless you first forgive them, you will always be chained to them through their offense.

EMT Marriages Matter

# CALL TO ACTION:

Write out a list of the three people from work that you have hard or hurt feelings over. Let's take it an honest step further; include anyone that you hate. Yes, hate against others we work with runs rampant among the hero fraternity.

Now begin to pray that you forgive each person. You don't have to tell those people that you forgive them unless you choose to, but what you must do is each day start to simply say, "God, I forgive _____ for _____." Commit to doing this until the hate in your heart is removed.

# **DAY 28**

Fighting Fair

*Death and life are in the power of the tongue, and those who love it will eat its fruits.*
*He who finds a wife finds a good thing and obtains favor from the Lord.*
*~ Proverbs 18:21-22*

Please practice speaking with kindness to each other. Leah and I call it, "Fighting Fair." Sure, I can out argue her and intimidate her into almost any decision I want through pure force of will and stubbornness.

But is that how God wants us to care for our spouse? A 2:24 Unit is about 2-as-1 for creating an invincible team as husband and wife.

God says the tongue holds the power of death and life. There's also no coincidence that the very next verse in Proverbs 18 talks about how a man who finds a wife is a good thing and a blessing from God.

This association is coupled together to illustrate how important it is for us to speak power into each other's life. I'm no different than EMTs in that we never enter a confrontation to lose. That used to be my mindset with Leah, but all it did was hurt her. She doesn't thrive on conflict and conquest. When I learned to fight fair, we immediately reached resolution rather than winner or loser.

It's also a reminder to us that we've been blessed with a wonderful gift from God in our spouse. The way we treat the gift reflects on how we feel about the gift giver. By caring for our spouse, we honor God. The first and best way to do that is through our words.

EMT Marriages Matter

# CALL TO ACTION:

When's the last time you said something harsh to your spouse? How about just a dry, cutting comment? It all hurts the same. As a kid, it was common to put a coin in the swear jar when we cursed. All that did was collect a lot of coins.

This isn't the same thing. Harsh words and fighting with the only person who is as much a part of us as we are to ourselves is also hurting us. Focus on your words.

Take a moment and run them through your mind before speaking if you have to, but take precautions to safeguard both of you from hurtful speech and unproductive arguments.

# DAY 29

Friends Are Rare

*For from day to day men
came to David to help him,
until there was a great army,
like an army of God.*
~ *1 Chronicles 12:22*

Friends actually play a major role in the building of a solid 2:24 Unit. True friends will support you both through good times and bad. Bad friends can't wait to see you miserable because why else; misery loves company.

Learning to foster sound, affirming friendships is very similar to the way we invest in our own marriage. Friendships require vulnerability. Without it, there can never be an intimacy between you. This is where the distinction of friends and acquaintances is most profound.

The latter have bonds of loyalty, mutual admiration and even sacrifice, but beyond occupational obligations, the absence of intimacy is where lines are drawn at the job, the gym or the gang who heads out for after-work happy hour.

Most of us purposely keep others at a stiff arms distance. Once we've been on the job a while, it also becomes the standard distance for family, parents and siblings, as well as anyone else. Men especially need other men as friends. But caution is key in determining who inspires you versus those who consume your energy and leave you drained.

We isolate ourselves, and while we may stand in formation with hundreds of brothers and sisters in blue, we are alone. But, friends are just a greeting and call away. Actually, there are lots of EMTs sitting at home alone right now, because of divorce, addiction, depression; who would give anything for a friend.

EMT Marriages Matter

# CALL TO ACTION:

This call to action opened my eyes years ago, and although it was painful, it helped me to understand the reality of friends. This really pertains to you men because we seem to have trouble opening up to friendship.

Write out a list of your friends. Do not include people you work with, or your spouse's friend who you only know because of them. Identify actual people you would confess your sin to without having to worry about them breaking your trust. If you have around five, consider yourself blessed. If you have between none and one, consider yourself an average adult.

# DAY 30

Freedom & Forgiveness

*Father, forgive them;*
*for they do not know what they are doing"*
*~ Luke 23:34*

Freedom through forgiveness is a radical challenge for us. We're used to holding grudges, waiting for the mystical karma, or handling business on our own.

We're not naturally inclined to tell on ourselves, nor are we quick to apologize. When we've offended our beloved, and failed or refused to apologize and ask forgiveness we leave wounds on their spirit.

Those injuries don't just go away. Remember this: time does not heal inner pain.

When apologies come easy because both of you trust that repair and restoration are the goal, the soft words short-circuit potential implosions. This safe shelter of communications is also a result of a shared mutual respect for each other.

Sometimes we set an expectation for our spouse that moves beyond self-improvement and into an unobtainable perfection. Without the mutual grace of forgiveness, spouses find themselves in an unenviable demigod position of do no wrong.

That shaky pedestal won't last, and because we're hesitant to confess when forgiveness is needed, we remain perched on a broken branch of selfish refusals and dangerous denial. A trusted place to seek forgiveness removes the hesitation of being seen as weak.

The only way you will grow an indestructible marriage is to assure each other that forgiveness for a confessed and repentant heart is the grace both will always offer each other.

EMT Marriages Matter

# CALL TO ACTION:

Today, both of you promise each other that there is a safe place to land in confession, and that each will be there to forgive and help the other one up. Forgiving is about freeing yourself from the offense against you. It doesn't approve of what the other person did, but it will open the door toward healing for both parties.

# DAY 31
Money Marriage

*The rich rule over the poor,*
*and the borrower is servant to the lender.*
*~ Proverbs 22:7*

Money is one of the most fought over issues in relationships. Next, blend two individuals from independent socioeconomic backgrounds, and you've got an epic blowout just waiting to occur.

## FAIR, NOT EQUAL

You must think in terms of fair, and not equal when it comes to dealing with every situation that requires money. Will you mix your money, or maintain separate bank accounts? Unless there are binding legal contracts, wills, heirship, or annuities preventing the commingling of monies, God's will for the union of two people entering into a heavenly covenant is for two to become one.

## ALL IN

While you may prosper financially, or just get by with paying the bills with two separate accounts, you're missing a spiritual blessing by not obeying God's word to blend.

There can be no a la carte of blending lives, kids, cash or debts. It's not realistic to say I'll blend the bedroom closet, but not your cash. No, it's all in.

When your money is just dating, it may have the tendency to venture out on its own expenditures, new people, or oppress your spouse. Chances are you earn different salaries. The one who makes more, but only chips in to match their spouse on bills, mortgage, education, etc. rules over them according to God's word. Relational inequity grinds against God's grain.

**I NOW INVEST YOU:**

- Combine all money accounts
- Work together on developing monthly budgets
- Set financial priorities
- Consult each other before big purchases
- Create realistic family financial goals
- Discuss money with children – appropriately
- Skip the Prenups

How Have You Blended Monies?

EMT Marriages Matter

# CALL TO ACTION:

Commit to not allowing money to control your marriage. Take immediate steps today to set a budget, boundaries and a vision for establishing the role of money as a resource in your relationship.

# DAY 32

Boundaries for Family

*If anyone will not welcome you
or listen to your words, leave that home or town
and shake the dust off your feet.*
~ *Matthew 10:14*

Good fences make good neighbors. Sometimes those fences are erected to protect you from your very own family. Directly or indirectly, toxic family and in-laws are a common cause of divorce.

Boundaries are there to protect what is valuable to you and your spouse. When you truly leave your blood family to cleave to your spouse, that family becomes secondary to your marriage.

The best way to set clear rules for preventing outside influence from causing harm is to create a Position Statement. This is a written guide that lists what you will and will not accept from others.

It may seem cold or harsh, but it is not a letter attacking or accusing any one person. It's simply a list of rules by which you abide and ask others to respect if they are to have a role in your life and marriage.

Both of you must communicate your Position Statement to family members. This guide is a living document that should be revisited often as life and relationships change.

## EXAMPLES:

- Interfering in faith and religious services of children (grandparents have been known to get kids baptized without parents' consent)
- Interfering in child rearing and if kids stay over with family, that they exercise same practice as when kids are at home. (diet, movies, use of car seats, etc.)

- Parents may spend holidays but not sleep in couple's home
- Giving money to their child to secret from spouse
- Giving child ultimatums (It's either your spouse or your family)

EMT Marriages Matter

# CALL TO ACTION:

Each of you draft out a position statement. Next, both of you work together to create the final document. Finally, discuss the best way to share this with all of your family and friends who hold an influence in your marriage.

# **DAY 33**

Surviving Debt

*Keep your lives free from the love of money
and be content with what you have,
because God has said,"Never will I leave you;
never will I forsake you."*
*~ Hebrews 13:5(NIV)*

Living with debt is a horribly dark, oppressive cloud that lurks over every aspect of your life. The worst life and money decisions we can make are those based on fear.

So many of us end up quitting our beloved public service careers to find other jobs that pay more per check but contribute nothing to pension, healthcare or deferred comp.

We know planning for a thirty-year retirement when you're over your head in debt is like giving a drowning man a glass of water, but long-term vision is a part of the process of regaining financial freedom and personal peace.

We're not going to reinvent the wheel. Based on scriptural principles and sound financial management, there are basic steps that include a commitment to take control of your money.

Don't be afraid of money. It will only hurt when you don't take control of it. Money also has a way of walking away unless you are responsible with it.

This isn't being stingy, it's about mature money management.

You must begin by working together to create a monthly budget. It's not hard to list what you make versus what you owe. If you owe more than you make, then killing down debt is your priority.

Adjustments in lifestyle often help free up money that can be paid toward your debt. Knocking out the small amounts and then rolling those payments to the next amount will soon show you that you can survive debt, but it takes a 2:24 Unit effort to break into financial freedom.

EMT Marriages Matter

## **CALL TO ACTION:**

Do you have a family budget? If not, begin the process of talking about the need to draft one. Identify your debt, live within your means and take the fear out of finances.

# DAY 34

I Forgive You

*I, even I, am He who blots out
your transgressions for My own sake;
and I will not remember your sins.*
~ Isaiah 43:25

The alpha culture of law enforcement often comes with the threats of preying upon each other to establish a professional pecking order.

Alphas have never experienced anything like being hazed until we become one of our nation's bravest. Then why is the unrelenting EMT culture harassment allowed? Because it's all alpha personalities who fight to establish dominance. If ascending to the top means throwing you under the bus, then so be it.

But getting thrown under a bus, actual or figurative, is painful. Try actively forgiving those who hurt you in the squad room, and you will see a major difference in the way you develop a spiritual immunity to their jabs and attacks.

You must work to forgive them no matter how hard it is. Trust us, it's not just you feeling the dump truck of interoffice anxiety. Your spouse and family suffer from it too. How? Because you come home and dump it on them.

Free yourself from those who cause you harm at work, and spare those you love at home. You've been through tough times and have learned to endure the struggle on the job. But, by forgiving, you now can break free from it.

"I forgive you."

EMT Marriages Matter

## CALL TO ACTION:

List three people who really get under your skin. Now begin the process of forgiving them. Yes, even if you whisper in the privacy of your car, _____, I forgive you. That's a start to unchaining yourself from the hurt and anger they cause you.

Now, the second part of the process is to bless those people. We know, it can be tough, but once you've been freed from them and understand that God also loves them, you will see that blessing them is the greatest gift God has given you. We always pray that God blesses them with salvation and someone to come into their lives to lead them there. Try it.

# PART 5 - MISSION ACCOMPLISHED

# DAY 35

Seeing Is Achieving

*"For I know the plans I have for you,"*
*declares the Lord,*
*"plans to prosper you and not to harm you,*
*plans to give you hope and a future."*
*~ Jeremiah 29:11*

**PRAISE**

Leah and I start every day off with prayer time. Some days are long, deeply emotional prayers as God moves us, and other mornings are quick words of praise and proclamations. We praise God no matter how bad we hurt or how strained our marriage may be.

Why? Because God is good for His word and no matter how horrible your life may have been in the past, you have always come out on the other side. Giving credit where credit is due will elevate your perspective to the good things in life.

## PROCESS

No matter how life looks, are you and your spouse sharing prayer time, setting a marriage vision and building the infrastructure to make your vision become reality?

It might be a new home, kids, getting out of debt, or a different job, but what matters most, is being purposeful about the process of gaining God's assured blessings.

I like the saying, "If you can see it, you can be it." Seeing doesn't mean having to actually lay eyes on something like spotting a bad guy through a sniper's scope. Believing without seeing is called faith, and it's the cornerstone to receiving the blessings you want to see.

## PROCLAIM

We help each other "see it" by making checklist and using that as a guide during our prayer time. Give it a try. Once you catch the vision, see how fast God helps your desires come into alignment with His provision. God will provide, but he's not like an old uncle at Christmas doling out cash. It requires faith.

Vision and Provision are spiritually linked so you can see God's hand at work. Catch the vision!!

EMT Marriages Matter

## CALL TO ACTION:

Are you both praying together with the full expectancy of God's blessing? Do you wonder if He hears you, or is going to answer your prayers?

Honestly, if you're not praying in His will to know His will and do His will, then you're spending time making a wish list. If you want a power-packed prayer list, begin to pursue God's desires for your heart and then pray with expectancy.

# DAY 36

Godly Loving

*And over all these virtues put on love, which binds them all together in perfect unity.*
*~ Colossians 3:1 (NIV)*

God has blessed you with the one person you were meant to spend the rest of your life with. That doesn't mean a magical soulmate, but it does mean a spiritual gift of having the capacity to show Godly love to your spouse.

Marriage is our treasure, so why wouldn't we take care of and nurture the gift God has given us? If the relationship with our spouse is healthy, we will be happy. It takes effort to love someone. Especially if they're not acting particularly lovable. And by consciously doing these things, we're setting ourselves up for a happy marriage.

1) Love God

When we love God, everything else falls into place. Our spouse will notice. Our children will notice. Loving God changes you, and it subsequently changes the people around you.

*Charm is deceptive, and beauty does not last; but a woman who fears the Lord will be greatly praised. Reward her for all she has done. Let her deeds publicly declare her praise.*
~ *Proverbs 31:30-31*

2) Respect Your Spouse

The number one thing men want is respect. And they really want it from their wives. If you want to see a change in your marriage or your husband, show him respect, even if you think he doesn't deserve it.

The most important thing to women is security. Your wife needs to know that they are in a love-filled, caring relationship. Security not only comes from physically protecting her, it also comes from showing her that you're willing to be vulnerable and understanding.

*So again I say, each man must love his wife*
*as he loves himself, and the wife*
*must respect her husband.*
*~ Ephesians 5:33*

3) Pray For Your Spouse

Have you ever heard the saying, "The couple that prays together, stays together?" I pray for Leah every single day, even days where I'm irritated with her or if we've had a fight.

I do it for two specific reasons:

1) Praying for her daily reminds me that my marriage is a priority, because it's easy to forget when life gets busy.

2) I want to be intentional in my prayers for her.

> *Therefore, confess your sins to one another and pray for one another, that you may be healed.*
> ~ *James 5:16*

## 4) Seek To Please Your Spouse in Intimacy

This is an important one. Physical intimacy in marriage is crucial. Becoming one brings us closer together and binds us like nothing else can. Sex is especially important to us men.

> *The husband should fulfill his wife's sexual needs, and the wife should fulfill her husband's needs.*
> ~ *1 Corinthians 7:3*

## 5) Learn To Forgive and Apologize Quickly

The key word there is quickly. You're going to have some fights that are real doozies. Sometimes you're going to be mad. Sometimes she's going to be mad. But at the end of the day you love each other. Don't waste your time holding grudges or giving the silent treatment.

I can't imagine there are a lot of widows or widowers in this world who would say if asked, "I wish we'd spent more hours fighting."

*God resists the proud
but gives grace to the humble.
James 4:6*

6) Keep Your Marriage Private

Build each other up. Never complain about your spouse to your friends, co-workers, or while waiting for a PTA meeting to start. This goes back to respect and security. Your friends, or anyone you complain to, will remember what you said and think poorly of your spouse long after you've moved past whatever had you complaining in the first place.

## 7) Forget the Past

Leah says this may be one of the most difficult things for women to do. Whether it's your husband's past before he met you or why you asked him to sleep on the couch six years ago, bringing up past transgressions when you're angry feeds your own sense of self-righteousness in why you're right.

Learn to forgive and learn to apologize, and mean it. Then move on.

## 8) Compliment Your Spouse

Compliment: *An expression of praise, commendation, or admiration.*

Tell your husband he's doing a good job as provider and protector of your family. Thank him when he fulfills your needs, whether it's something as simple as letting you sleep in one morning or rubbing the sore spot in your back. Appreciate him, and then *tell* him you appreciate him.

Tell your wife that you love her, and that you'd marry her today if you did it all over again. Thank her and encourage her for the things she does for you. Even if it's holding you back to protect you from tumbling forward. Practice non-sexual intimate touching to express that being physical doesn't always have to lead to sex. She'll appreciate that!

It's our *honor* to be the greatest support system each other will ever have.

## 9) Divorce is NOT an Option

Go into your marriage with the idea that divorce isn't an option. That attitude gives your spouse confidence that no matter what goes wrong between you, that you'll still be married and still love each other at the end of it.

EMT Marriages Matter

## CALL TO ACTION:

Pray over this list and honestly identify which ones you are and are not doing. Ask yourself why it is that you are not doing some and are doing others. Is it because there's unforgiven sin or anger between the two of you that is stopping you from opening yourself up completely?

# DAY 37

Active Listening

*Just then, as Pilate was sitting on the judgment seat, his wife sent him this message: "Leave that innocent man (Jesus) alone. I suffered through a terrible nightmare about him last night."*
~ *Matthew 27:19*

There is no coincidence that Pilate's wife, Claudia was highlighted in Matthew 27:19. It's one of the most critical times in all of history, and one man had one chance to heed his wife's words. Pilate, who was considered a righteous man, suffered as a result of his decision.

Learning to actively listen is a skill most men aren't born with, but it is something to be honed. It's often more helpful than men realize. Gathering of information of any form is always a bonus.

A man's desire to bypass the eighty page instruction manual and fix it not only delays getting it fixed, but it fails to show your wife that you're willing to work as a team even if it means listening to instructions.

Take the time to pray God will change you to be a better listener. Give true, purposeful listening a try. These are a few reasons why it's so critical to listen to your wife.

1. It shows love and respect.
2. It helps you to see a full perspective in a given situation.
3. It shows your patience and wisdom.
4. It teaches your sons how to value a woman and their future wife by honoring her words.
5. It shows your daughters how to expect to be treated and honored by men and her future husband.
6. It reveals the Christ in you.

Each is a unique gift from God, crafted specifically by the Creator of life to complement each other. Communication is God's way of fellowshipping with us, and it's His way for us to intimately know each other. Give active listening a try.

EMT Marriages Matter

# CALL TO ACTION:

Focus the time to sit and talk with each other. More importantly, focus on listening, hearing and processing what each other says. Try relaying back to your spouse, "What you are saying is…" or "This is how I interpret what you just said…"

We know, it's not a normal pattern of communications, but it will emphasize the point of transmitting, receiving, interpreting and responding. You might be surprised by what you hear.

# DAY 38
Leading Equally

*Husbands, love your wives, just as Christ loved the church and gave himself up for her.*
*~ Ephesians 5:25*

God created marriage.

This union of marriage, whether yours is good or bad, was not the invention of a politician or attorney. Nor was it imagined by some social media influencer. From the very beginning of beginnings, marriage was created by God. That design requires order just like everything to survive and thrive. Part of that order is in our marital roles. This isn't outdated or obsolete. It's eternal.

Yet, people become indifferent when words like surrender, submission and servant are used. Suddenly, we've adopted a moral superiority superseding God's design. Terms like surrender, submission and service are not negative words to the selfless servant. Take a look at the Navy SEALs for example. Do you see them as weak? Of course not, but they must surrender their authority to a chain-of-command and submit to training, discipline and mentoring before they are allowed to earn the honor of wearing the SEAL trident. Only then, are they presented to serve.

It's no different with marriage. I believe the challenge comes from not identifying the difference between leadership and headship. The husband and wife are completely equal. Although God created Adam first, He created Eve equal. This is where leadership is shared equally between you two.

The missing element in most discussions about roles in marriage is found in headship. God designated man as the spiritual head of his family. This does not equal leader, boss, better or first. Headship is a gender specific assignment of responsibility. It's a spiritual designation requiring men to love their wives.

Ephesians 5 is where we stumble if we're looking to stumble. But, in the context of understanding that you are both equal and leaders, nowhere does God appoint man as the boss. He demands that husbands love their wives and as the spiritual head of that union, be willing to give himself up for her as Christ does for His bride the church.

I'm not sure about you, but those very words people get so upset about when they misrepresent them as applying to only woman – surrender, submission and servant also apply directly to men too.

EMT Marriages Matter

## CALL TO ACTION:

What are you each good at? Leah is the money manager in our home, while I'm better at initiating activities for the family. It doesn't mean either are less than the other, it just means God blessed us with different gifts.

Take time to talk with each other about the areas in your marriage where God has gifted you. Identify those strengths, and focus on supporting and developing them in each other.

# **DAY 39**

Things Love Changes

*Therefore, if anyone is in Christ,
he is a new creation. The old has passed away;
behold, the new has come.*
~ *2 Corinthians 5:17*

Let's scrap the old saying that you can't teach an old dog new tricks. Love and marriage is unlike anything we could've ever known. And besides, this isn't about tricks.

I'd been divorced almost twenty years before Leah and I met and married. I was an old dog and had accumulated a mixed bag of tricks. But one thing was certain. If I wanted to enter into and remain in a rock solid 2:24 Unit marriage, I couldn't bring that old baggage along on a new journey. The choice to love is also the choice to change.

The love we come to know through marriage is the best of love as God designed it to be shared between each other. Here are a few of love's positive effects:

1. Physical Changes – Love has physiological effects on your body. Chemical levels such as dopamine, testosterone, norepinephrine, histocompatibility complex (MHC), and pheromones shift. These are all positive benefits.

2. Perspective – Love shifts your self-centered worldview into a shared, or partner-focused lens. Learning to see the world through another person's heart is a powerful experience. It becomes a more transparent process as trust and love deepens.

3. Fighting Clean – Single people fight for one thing; preservation for their way of life. Throw a monkey wrench in their

machinery and they come out fighting like an angry cat mistakenly bathed by a toilet's flush. Love softens the heart for considering someone else's point of view, and the potential for understanding that the world really doesn't revolve around you.

4. Sexier Sex – Intimacy and trust lead to increased sexual pleasure. While being single and ready to mingle might make for a great beer commercial campaign, the reality of lonely nights, untrustworthy partners, or revolving door relations eventually leads to sexual dissatisfaction.

5. A Better You – Let's face it, when it's only you that you have to please, becoming self-consumed is almost guaranteed. Without outside stimuli, rare is the occasion to grow or improve. Because it is God's expressed will that two people should become one, it's not only pleasing

to Him, but immeasurably pleasing to you.

EMT Marriages Matter

# CALL TO ACTION:

Commit the time to talk with each other to identify what else being married has made better. Our expectation is that the first item on your list would be each other!

# DAY 40

Happily Married

*He who finds a wife finds a good thing,*
*And obtains favor from the Lord.*
*~ Proverbs 18:22 (NKJV)*

Being married is a great gift. Being happily married is the best gift on earth. Too often marriage becomes the backdrop instead of the focus. Trust us when we share that making your marriage the top spot in your life will not take away from anything else that is amazing. It will always and only intensify everything else around it. One truth that we hope you will always remember is if you want your marriage to be important, you must treat it like it's important. No championship rings for second place efforts. It's all in, all of the time. The reward will be greater than you ever imagined.

There is no peace in the world like that of sharing an open, honest and transparent relationship with your spouse. When there are no secrets or hidden darkness lurking to destroy you, every day can be lived with full assurance of knowing that your 2:24 Unit is there no matter what else goes down in the job or in life.

EMTs don't have the luxury of peace and consistency, but in a rock solid marriage, it doesn't matter what the winds dust up; our waters run deep and remain still in the worst of times. That soulful wisdom comes as a result of an intimate and intentional relationship with your spouse and a faith in God.

We are so proud of you for working through these 40 days to a better EMT marriage. Whether you went at it alone, or together, what is important is that you made the commitment to make your marriage work. One spouse praying for the other is a powerful weapon against marital chaos, so never underestimate the effectiveness of faithful prayer.

Leah and I are so thankful for your marriage's sacrifice to service, and your passion for the 2:24 unit. We are praying over you both and know that God is waiting to honor and bless you covenant with Him and your spouse. Marriage Rocks!

God bless you!

> EMT Marriages Matter,
> Chief Scott and Leah Silverii

# AFTERWORD

You made it!

Whether you and your spouse worked through each day, you took turns, or only one of you took the lead, what's important is that your marriage was represented.

Leah and I wanted to cover some of the most common hot-button topics in marriage. We call them the marriage killers, and the best way to divorce proof your relationship is to be aware of the dangers that lurk in the dark waiting to ambush you.

Now that you know, there's a much better success rate for tackling those threats head-on as opposed to being sucker punched. We want you to enjoy a healthy, happy marriage as God created it to be. You're now 40 steps closer to having that relationship of your dreams.

Please know that we've prayed over every day and for every couple who have cared enough to invest in their marriage. God will bless you, and sustain you even in the most trying of times. All you have to do is have faith.

Sometimes that faith requires active prayer, unlimited forgiveness or showing undeserved grace, but God always has your six. Never give up on marriage because God will never give up on you.

EMT Marriages Matter,
Chief Scott and Leah Silverii

# ACKNOWLEDGMENTS

When we started thinking of everyone who has played a part in what has become this devotional, we realize what a special community is involved in 1st Responder marriage ministry.

Leah and I are blessed to stand the gap with so many friends who supported us in marriage and now support each other in the battle to strengthen and save EMT marriages.

Thank you to Dar Albert at Wicked Smart Designs and Kim Cannon for all your work on making this book a reality.

EMT Marriages Matter,
Chief Scott and Leah Silverii

# ABOUT THE AUTHORS

Dr. Scott Silverii and his wife, Leah, have blended seven kids and a French bulldog named Bacon into a wonderfully unique family. Their passion is helping hurting marriages.

They're the founders of Blue Marriage, a first responder marriage ministry that created the Police Marriage Academy. They are both certified as Marriage On The Rock counselors and SYMBIS facilitators.

Scott, a retired chief of police, holds a PhD from the University of New Orleans and is working toward his Doctor of Ministry at The King's University. Leah is a New York Times and USA Today bestselling author of over 65 titles.

When not spending time with their kids, they enjoy crossing the country on their motorcycle, or hanging out with friends in their hometown of Dallas, Texas.

An experienced speaker, mentor and confidential accountability partner, Scott and Leah are available for workshops, conferences, and church events. Their complete line of resources can be found at Silverii Ministry - www.silveriiministry.com.

*Let's Connect*

# OTHER BOOKS BY SCOTT AND LEAH

**The Bro Code Series**
Bro, Man Up
Bro, Keep It In Your Pants
Bro, You Free?
Bro, Stay Free
Bro Code Daily Devotional

**Stand Alone Titles**

Broken and Blue: A Policeman's Guide To Health, Hope, and Healing
Life After Divorce: Finding Light In Life's Darkest Season
Police Organization and Culture: Navigating Law Enforcement in Today's Hostile Environment
The ABCs of Marriage: Devotional and Coloring Book

# A First Responder Devotional

40 Days to a Better Firefighter Marriage
40 Days to a Better Military Marriage
40 Days to a Better Corrections Officer Marriage
40 Days to a Better 911 Dispatcher Marriage
40 Days to a Better EMT Marriage
40 Days to a Better Police Marriage

www.ingramcontent.com/pod-product-compliance
Lightning Source LLC
Chambersburg PA
CBHW052055110526
44591CB00013B/2224